3

Marco hears his friend being bullied.

How can Marco be a good citizen?

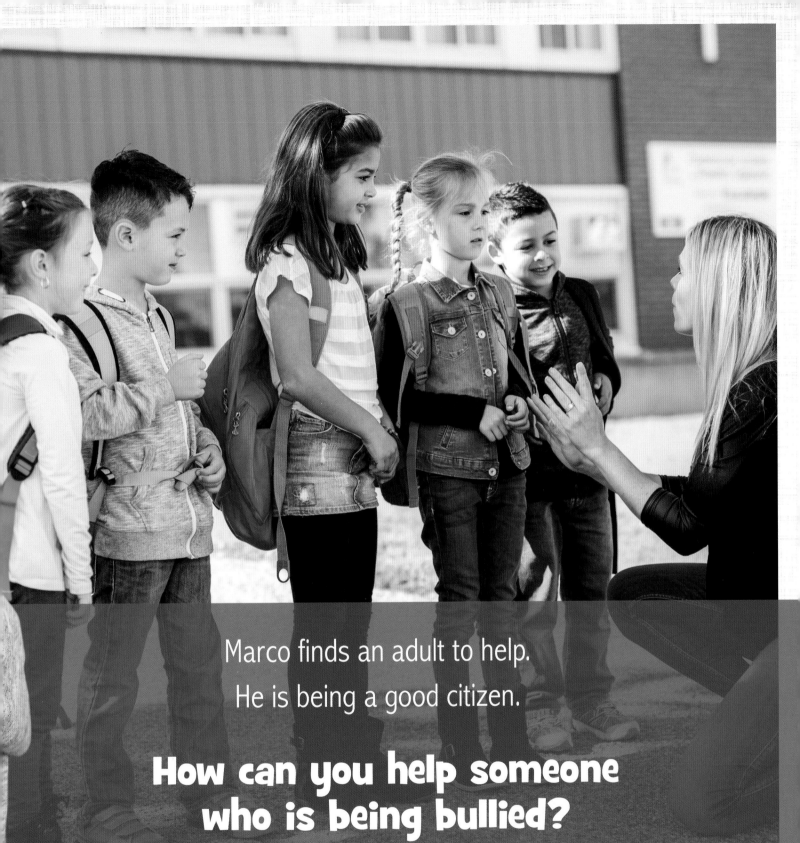

Marco finds an adult to help.
He is being a good citizen.

How can you help someone who is being bullied?

Noah thinks the lake near his home should be cleaner.

How could Noah be a good citizen?

How to Be a
GOOD
CITIZEN

A Question and Answer Book About Citizenship

by Emily James

Members of a community are called citizens.

Being a good citizen means working to make your community a better place.

It also means helping to make
the world a better place.
There are lots of ways to be a good citizen.

Noah and his sister learn about the environment and find ways to help.

Noah is being a good citizen.

How could you help the environment?

Lucy goes to the library.
She borrows two new books.

**How can Lucy
be a good citizen?**

8

Lucy takes good care of the books. She respects the library's property. She is also being a good citizen.

How can you show respect for someone else's things?

A new family has moved next door to Kate.

What can Kate do to be a good citizen?

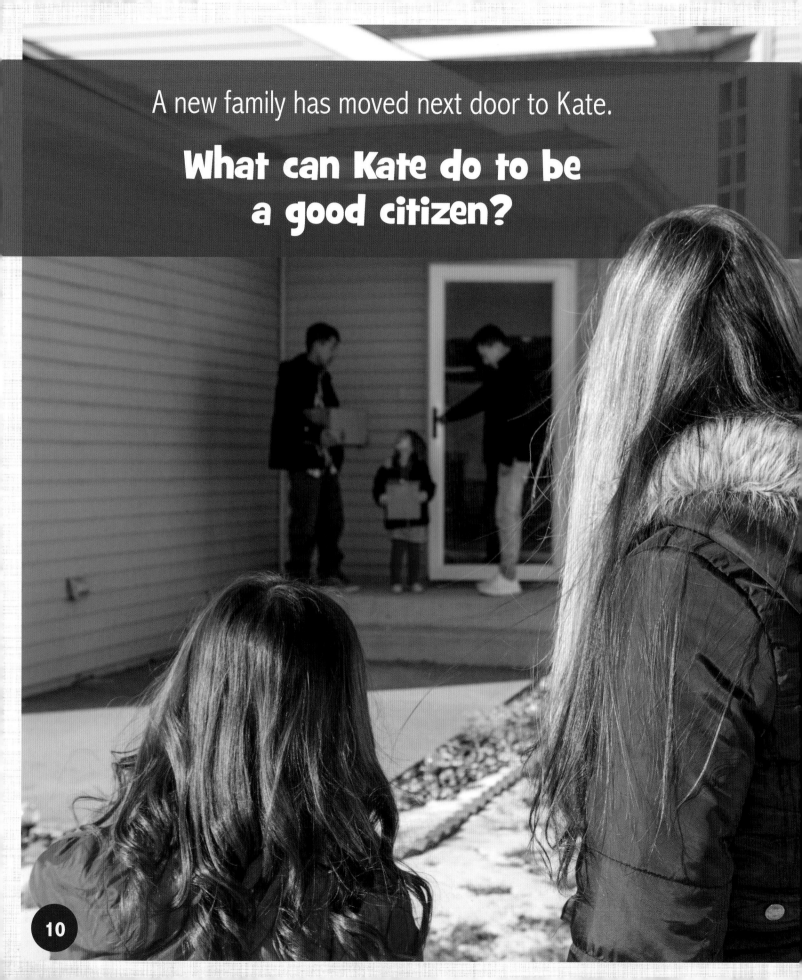

Kate visits the family to say hello. She welcomes new people to her community. She is also being a good citizen.

How could you help someone new feel welcome?

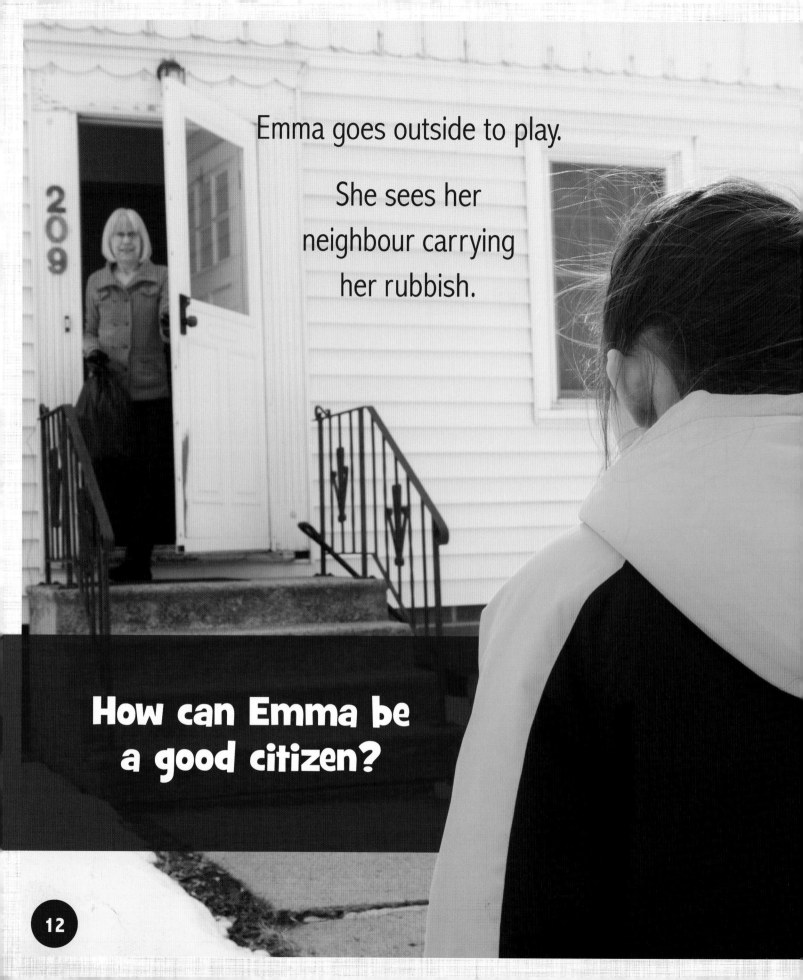

Emma goes outside to play.

She sees her neighbour carrying her rubbish.

How can Emma be a good citizen?

Emma helps her neighbour take the bin bag to the pavement. Being a good citizen means being a good neighbour.

How can you be a good neighbour?

Olivia spots some litter
on the floor.

How can Olivia be
a good citizen?

Olivia picks up the litter. She puts it in the rubbish bin. Good citizens don't drop litter. They help keep the community clean.

What can you do to keep your community clean?

Election day is coming up. People need to know about the candidates.

How can Colin be a good citizen?

Colin helps his mum hand out flyers. He hopes adults will vote. Good citizens vote in elections.

What can you do to help at election time?

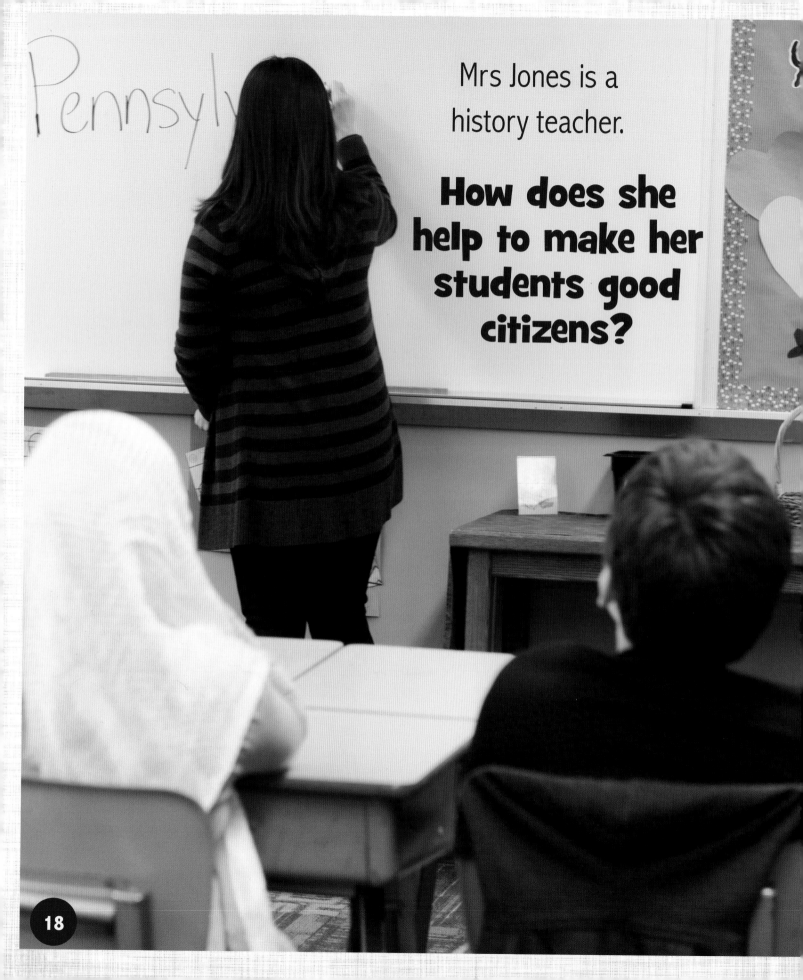

Mrs Jones is a history teacher.

How does she help to make her students good citizens?

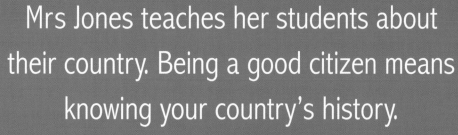

Mrs Jones teaches her students about their country. Being a good citizen means knowing your country's history.

What do you know about your country's history?

Nina has a lot of toys.
She doesn't have time to
play with them all.

**How can Nina be
a good citizen?**

Nina gives some of her toys away.
Good citizens donate to charity.

What are some
other things
you could give
to charity?

DONATE

Omar wants to ask his teacher a question.

He knows the rule is to put up his hand.

What should Omar do to be a good citizen?

Omar puts up his hand before speaking.
Good citizens follow rules.

What are some important rules that you follow?

Maria and Levi want to make their neighbourhood look nice.

What can they do to be good citizens?

Maria and Levi plant flowers.

Good citizens make the world a better place.

What can you do to make the world a better place?

Gunner has ideas to improve his school.

What can Gunner do to be a good citizen?

Gunner can be on the school council.
Good citizens are leaders.

In what ways can you be a leader?

Ethan knows some people in his community are in need.

How can Ethan be a good citizen?

Ethan volunteers to help pack food
for homeless people.
Good citizens help those in need.

How can you help someone in need?

Glossary

candidate a person who wans to be elected, such as a Member of Parliament

charity a group that raises money or collects goods to help people in need

citizen a member of a country or community who has the right to live there

donate to give something as a gift to a charity or cause

election the process of choosing someone or deciding something by voting

environment all of the trees, plants, water and soil

volunteer to offer to do something without pay

Comprehension questions

1. How is Marco a good citizen when he hears his friend being bullied?

2. Volunteering is one way you can be a good citizen. What does it mean to volunteer? Hint: Use your glossary for help!

3. Can you think of a time you were a good citizen? What did you do?

Find out more

Books

How Should I Behave?, Mick Manning and Brita Granstrom (Franklin Watts, 2017)

I Can Help (My Behaviour), Liz Lennon (Franklin Watts, 2015)

What Does it Mean to be British?, Nick Hunter (Raintree, 2017)

Websites

bbc.co.uk/education/topics/zw339j6/resources/1
Find lots of videos showing how you can be responsible in many different ways.

bbc.co.uk/education/clips/z8587hv
Watch a video to show how you can help care for the environment.

Index

Raintree is an imprint of Capstone Global Library Limited, a company incorporated in England and Wales having its registered office at 264 Banbury Road, Oxford, OX2 7DY – Registered company number: 6695582

www.raintree.co.uk
myorders@raintree.co.uk

Text © Capstone Global Library Limited 2018
The moral rights of the proprietor have been asserted.

ISBN 978 1 4747 4385 3 (hardcover)
21 20 19 18 17
10 9 8 7 6 5 4 3 2 1

ISBN 978 1 4747 4390 7 (paperback)
22 21 20 19 18
10 9 8 7 6 5 4 3 2 1

British Library Cataloguing in Publication Data
A full catalogue record for this book is available from the British Library.

Acknowledgements
Capstone Studio/Karon Dubke. except:
Shutterstock: Alinute Silzeviciute, 24, 25, Lopolo, 4, 5, Poznukhov Yurly, 6, 7, RoyStudioEU throughout, (background texture).

Editorial Credits
Jaclyn Jaycox, editor; Heidi Thompson, designer; Jo Miller, media researcher; Laura Manthe, production specialist; Marcy Morin, scheduler

Every effort has been made to contact copyright holders of material reproduced in this book. Any omissions will be rectified in subsequent printings if notice is given to the publisher.

All the Internet addresses (URLs) given in this book were valid at the time of going to press. However, due to the dynamic nature of the Internet, some addresses may have changed, or sites may have changed or ceased to exist since publication. While the author and publisher regret any inconvenience this may cause readers, no responsibility for any such changes can be accepted by either the author or the publisher.

Printed and bound in India.